we have grown together

Satyakam Sengupta

INDIA • SINGAPORE • MALAYSIA

ISBN
Paperback 979-8-89544-257-9
Hardcase 979-8-89544-833-5

we have grown together

To
My mother,
wife,
sisters and daughter

CONTENT

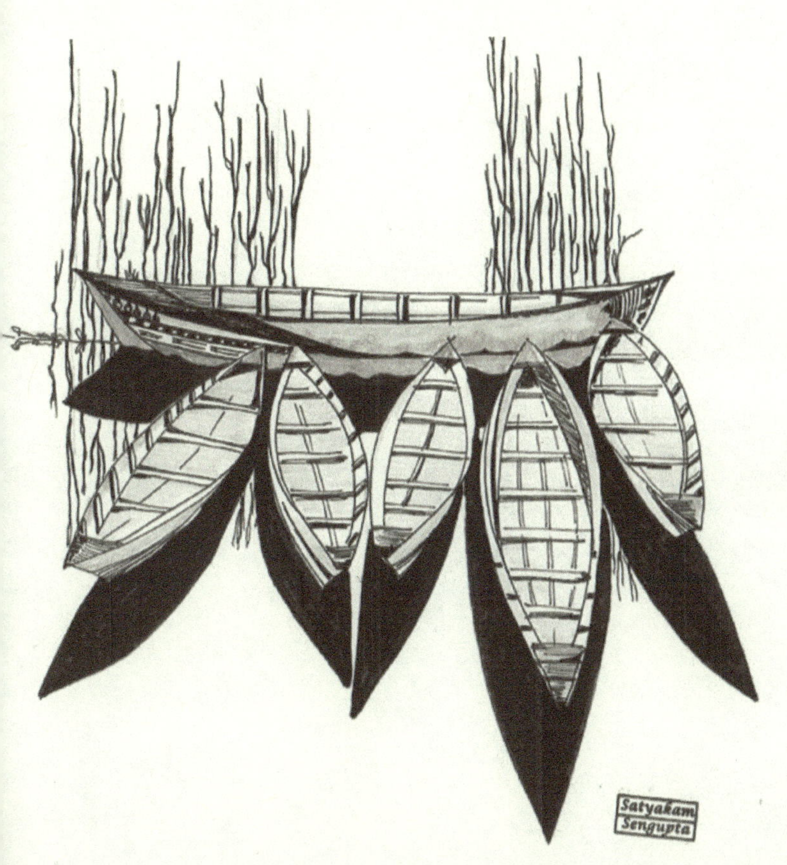

Satyakam
Sengupta

Introduction

What does one write about a person with whom one has spent more than half of one's life? Brought up in the rural ambience of ...mkum in erstwhile Bihar, the 'greens' seem to have 'seeped' into his ...ng. Even now he can 'smell' the advent of spring in the city air. His ...oto frame is ever-ready to capture the sparkling dew drop on the edge ...a leaf, the shimmering magic of a spider's web in the soft light of the ...ing sun and the restless ringlets of foam drawing patterns on the ...ore.

An Honours graduate from Narendrapur Ramakrishna Mission, he ...er went on to complete his Masters from the University of Calcutta. A ... in the banking sector did help to satisfy his material needs, but the ...ture of the job left behind a deep hunger in his mind which ultimately ...aded him into seeking premature retirement in order to find time to ...e vent to his vibrant imagination.

Publishing his book of poems has been a long-cherished dream. His ...etches interspersed with the poems, will surely intrigue his readers. ...e quality of his creativity is for the world to judge, but the number of ...ople equally adept at wielding the pen and the brush happen to be few ...d far between. May his dreams find fruition with the blessings of ...e Omnipresent!

...rth 24 Parganas   Bhaswati Sengupta (nee Bhaduri)
... May 2016

Acknowledgement

This small book of verse was a dream till yesterday. Now it is a reality. It took me a number of years to put it in place, as my service left me a little time to indulge in my creative pursuits.
The collection is arranged into four distinctive layers, viz, love confessions, songs of yesteryears, the world at large and remembrances.

The poems are mostly interspersed with my realizations and feelings though certain concepts expressed by my near and dear ones may find a place here and there. My mind has often wandered from one theme to another; the most recurrent being the sweet and sour tribulations of 'love', its confessions and the turmoil of this 'world at large'. The 'songs of yesteryears' and 'remembrances' are also associated with the passage of time; years of growing up and losses suffered.

I thank my wife Bhaswati for her gracious gesture, in writing the introduction for this book and sharing her thoughts and suggestions with me. The whole exercise has been possible for her unstinted support and cooperation. She has been a constant source of inspiration for me.

May 2016   Satyakam Sengupta

Satyakam
Sengupta

Foreword

i do not care
i repeat i just do not care
whether my verse has any merit or flair
whether it is structurally correct or looks bare
whether words are proper or fair
whether the couplets rhyme or pair
and whether whatever i declare
is universally rare or just a mere fare

i write what i dream and dare
and solemnly bid you to read and share
and at length toss up a silent prayer
for my infirmity and old-age care
there is many a poet
hidden from the human stare
the only challenge is that words get rare
and sometimes very hard to ensnare

i wish i could have done much better
if i possessed the cerebral power
to steal cupfuls of strewn nectar
of Sire Rabi's literary splendour
so that i could have given you all
a lot more enchanting verse to enthrall
which gradually spreads all over my soul

satyakam sengupta

love confessions

you left me with so much pain

you left me
with so much pain,

even after all these years
when the clock chimes three,
i consciously fear
that i may wantonly veer
to touch you dear,
and beg for sweet pardon
and reverse the years .....

sadly there was no one
at that wretched hour,

to appear and talk sense
in my flaming ears,
i never guessed
that the sun
would so quickly melt,
and the swans hurriedly
fly back to their realm .....

i sit by the raging sea
toying with crumpled dreams,

trying my level best
to find release from grief,
and live through
the silent passage of
merciless time,
melancholy enlarge and creep
from morning into deep night.....

i search for you
evermore eternally,
through dark corridors
and bylanes of history,
and fail to remember
that you are actually
by my side,

the waves roar
and the salt wipes out my sight,

should i find you,
when i forgetfully
put my mud-baked hands,
inside trouser pockets
of that promised land,
i would still love to caress
your tiny fingers,
spread over eons of naked
and wafting years,

and then love me as you will .....

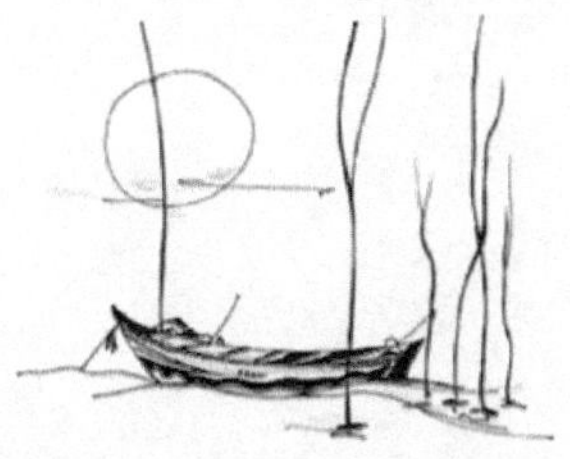

Satyakam
Sengupta

a gust of wind

when i need you most
by my side,
to light up my days, you are not there.

i had so much to say,
but could not say,
as you did not have the time to spare.

and whenever
we sat down together,
there sprung some nasty weather,
which gave you the plea,
to disappear.

don't ever say
i did not warn you,
of me fading in the wilderness,
you never had the patience,
to assess.

...... the gust of wind gathers in the air .....

now, after all these years,
He only knows,
what you hold dear,
or what you try to prove hereafter.

about me, i can say,
my dreams no longer laugh,
walk or stay,
they are all shattered and taken to decay.

you may feign forgetfulness

you may feign
forgetfulness now
but i remember the day
when you were by my side
trying to hold me tight
your soft fingers
nestling in mine

your breath
has embraced me
time and again
with the fresh waft
of ripening grains
your eyes have always shone
with ever-increasing radiance
of our eternal unison

your heart still pulsates
like bursting stars
on the balustrades
of my heart
often i am stirred
from my stupor
sudden ..... yet alert

how can you betray now
albeit your solemn vows
they cannot lie tossed
in the throes of biting frost
with no signs of
shame or crime

i wait and watch
for that delightful hour
when the soft screech of tyres
gradually manoeuvre
to release me
from the gnawing fire

this trauma can only cease
when you eventually finish
with the daily grind
of your restless life
smeared
with misplaced beliefs

this is a game
i never chose to play
but time
has its own course prepared
to subtly steer us away
from loved needs and desires

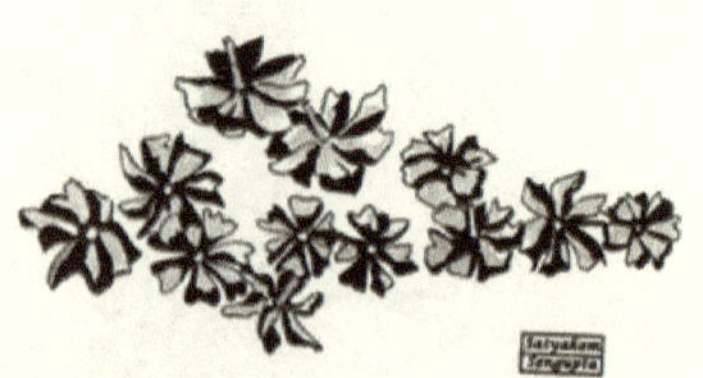

missgivings

why did you leave me?
in the raw cold
of a steely night ...

why didn't you whisper
sweet words?
to lift up my drowning spirits ...

why did you choose to
ruin my pride?
when i was not there to stop thee ...

oh! why did you choose to
want me?
when i didn't want to touch thee ...

the embryo of misgivings,
thrive, sigh and laze,
and bask under
subconscious shades
of worn out wooden gates ...

the answer scripts,
are willfully lost
in shelves of deceit and frost,
you are not here
to cleanse anymore, to care anymore ...

Satyakam
Sengupta

classroom walls

she stood behind
the classroom door,
eyelids brimming
with tidal bore,
watching our names
scribbled and greasy,
on fluttering flakes,
of peeling yore;

they timidly wait,
for an opportune date,
to spread silent wings,
and flee in the air,
scoffing at the
ever-widening chasm,
of gloom and despair;

the glow of love,
does not filter anymore,
the burning teardrops,
do not blister anymore,
and grief sustains,
a cold and lame broth,
of painful afterthoughts;

my palms turn red,
wet with prickly thorns,
of failing promises, and
a soul forlorn,
now the softness of her breath,
fails to heal me,
or play a song,
to soothe me asleep.

i am spent and am fazed,
at the misty haze,
swiftly drawing near,
to don me
with spreading disgrace,
and erase,
whatever little praise,
we amassed among friends;

i beat a retreat,
to shield my hide,
from the thundering sky,
my slippers are wet,
my shorts drenched,
the fairy-tale whistles
to disappear into the night,
and the shroud of ruin,
besieges me trust once again.

yet, do not dither
to summon me dear
if you ever sit and cry,
do not hesitate
to whisper me name
if you are ever tired and wry,

i may yet comfort thee
as i am still sufficiently left
with a constant heart
in my sty.

time's a-changing

i pray,
i'm able to see,
the flowers lift up their
heads with glee;

and dance joyously,
without mocking me;

and every nuzzling bee,
murmur collectively;

words of sweet happiness,
in my silent reverie;

i let the shackled dreams,
sweep down the slopes,
and flee;

and try to instill,
life's little treasure
of love,
in all for free;

however,
the pangs of parting,
have withered;

and the tiny rivulet of hopes,
have naively slithered,
into someone else's
backyard;

i do not search for thee,
anywhere, anymore,
my dear.

monsoon & mangoes

the monsoon
keeps tapping,
on the ivories
of my graying rooftop,
i watch the
steaming glow,
meekly overflow
the earth;

the teeming mob
of billows,
swarming my heaven,
peddles the potion
of love,
to almost
all the maidens ...

my love quietly
evaporates,
inside the rush-hour
traffic snarl,
seated in her
fragile blue chariot,
anxiously clutching
at her heart;

and the sweltering
bubble of dust,
whips-up
her pretty visage,
she never listens
to my entreaties,
of igniting
the ac in the air ...

she leaves me
stranded,
in the thick whirlpool
of passing chores,
and fetid market stores,
blaring music,
and the dreary throes
of nonstop bores;

they ebb up my skin,
to creep above
me knees,
slicing the impulse
of sweet harmony...

yet come summer,
come shower,
i need to fetch mangoes,
for my flower,
as she loves them
most at this hour;

i beat the indolence,
of my waning power,
to walk an extra mile,
and acquire
the decisive wager,
cause this
may be the only manner,
whereby she'll tolerate,
me in her bower ...

the lonesome glows

your fragrant head,
lay on my uneasy bed,
whispering words
of sweet love 'n joyous wonder,
of we two coming hither,
once more together,
and tie the perennial knot
a wee bit stronger,

but, the lonesome glows
of our tender vows,
softly march by us
in several rows,
i suffer,
the seizures of rejection,
on dual scores,

even now i hear,
your throbbing heart
trying to seal my ears,
the stifled stammers,
and the sighs of looming years,
the freezing clatter of filthy slander,
prolonged with the smack
of caustic laughter.

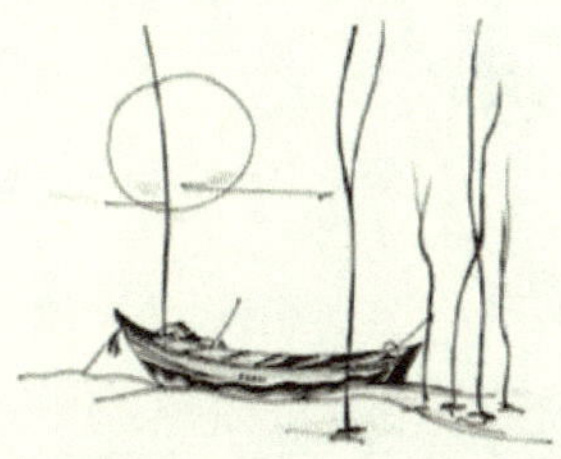

Satyakam
Sengupta

flowers adrift

my little flower
from rolling hills,
you know not still,
how realization reveals,
and inspiration
drives me wild.

i should have stirred
to reconcile,
and stopped to walk
those extra miles.

it is torture, it is pain,
to find and lose yer dimes
all over again,
desire, just hold on
don't expose the flame,
let us remain.

unhappiness, was it
just a passing phase,
or an aftermath
of some nameless malaise,
yet, thanks i say,
though teras nurse me,
through cheerless days.

however,
i do not mind this time,
it is definitely
not in mere whim or guise,
but in real earnest
you apologize,
by bidding me farewell,
with a concealed smile.

so no more drifting,
is that right .....

chimes

the merry pulse
of informal warmth,
stops beating
with the hum of rushing footfalls,
the chimes tinkle no more,
and the hour of existence
is overwhelmed,
by a bleak emotional overflow.

now, tea-cups rattle
echoing sporadic death knells,
of quiet intimacies,
you stand by my doorway,
trying to swear and say,
never to be
haughty 'n vain and go astray.

yet, the long hours
fail to predict the same,
though it begets a weird delight,
to brood night after night,
on what you'd be,
when armed in
one of your aggressive reveries.

preserved, you ought to be
not in bare halls cheap 'n bleak,
or like inert butterflies,
on glossy mounting bricks,
but in adoring hearts
gifted in scattering paradise,
whenever and wherever,
you ask for it.

impatience

patient, yes i always am,
and it is truly conveyed
by your friends,
yet patience and impatience
often merge,
in this turbulent transience
of youthful surge,
and at times it may breach,
the fragile bonds
of sobriety and trust.

but then, this is no answer
for you to choose,
it's better
to weep and cleanse,
and set your heaviness loose,
than flee the blazing barbs
of human stings,
and broken hearts,
'cause they have a habit
of bouncing back,
to cause more harm.

songs of yesteryears

fresh expressions

do i glimpse a flicker
of fresh hope,
in the shifting teardrop,
floating on the brink
of your eyes,

or is it a drop
of glistening moisture,
dripping down
rustling leaves,
swaying in the sky .....

now time is engraved
as polished gems,
in the
retreating chords,
of adolescent games,

every now and then,
i believe i see,
what i shouldn't see,
and all too often
haste destroys,
the nascent sparks
in the darkening sky .....

the rock and smoke,
is seized
with the stink,
of smothered ghosts,
and hapless force,

and the fierce itch
to elope knocks,
at her
bosoms core,
i'm baffled for more,
at the misty sight
of an open door,
ajar in the sky.....

broken promises

broken promises
smudge,
the frosty facades
of timid infatuations,
and prick the halo
of dying heart burns ...

broken promises
split and crash,
on swirling waters
of turbulent emotions,
echoing throbs
the size of demons ...

broken promises
smear awful pain,
on desolate farewells,
melting slowly
in the muggy terrain,
of chaos and disdain ...

broken promises
lie quietly tossed,
behind soiled handrails,
of disillusion and shame,
never to wake up
and join my game ...

magic wand

the church spires snooze,
amidst the hum
of nestling cuckoos,
i lift my fingers
in the fragile air,
to trace the benign refrain,
gently floating
from the morning prayers,
gliding breathlessly, o'er our
noiseless shadows,
lessening over rolling greens,
and passing meadows.

somewhere,
in the shuffling shade,
of shimmering greens,
sweet melodies,
of waltzing bulbuls
and humming bees,
fling open mystic corridors,
of celestial light,
abuzz with cheering gopis,
churning blissful games,
of unquenched tales.

i graze and gaze,
and am a man possessed,
inside the blessed embrace,
of blissful time,
the flute is no less,
than a magic wand,
which unites the soul,
with the cosmic whole,
it sings of known,
and unknown beauty,
and the essence,
of all-embracing energy.

my mind is calm at last,
in the chapel of
the sprawling hut,
where divine light,
still encircles the altar white,
nudging me steadily,
into ever increasing
whirlpools of profundity,
and i watch all reunite,
to sing His praise.

the great divide

sorrow

you have
enough reasons
to fret and weep

i did not
loosen the tender grip

it was you

who chose
to sign
the parting slip

now
let the salt
embalm thy wounds

and heal
the heart
that made mine bleed

Satyakam
Sengupta

burning scars

i watch the universe
play hide'n seek,
with million stars,
over my heaving breast,
now thick with
burning scars.

loneliness creeps
like serpents,
all over me bones,
as a soulmate,
chooses to build it's nest
elsewhere on its own.

the winged gods
do not perceive,
and do not volunteer
to avert the blunder,
and cease my infamy.

neither do they demolish,
the canon of my desires,
nor do they light the fire,
to extinguish
my ghoulish ire.

inevitably,
wicked beliefs,
are destined to spawn,
in this smog of gloom,
humid, and rancid dawn.

they move
ahead and on,
as seeds are freely sown,
and none can envisage,
the final strain
of the ripening corn.

nature has its own way
of playing tricks,
with life-building bricks,
leaving no space
to wipe the froth,
that sprouts
all, ill-begotten rot.

i'm sorry, i could'nt win,
the silver streaks
of joy and calm,
so that i could play hide'n seek,
with million stars,

over my heaving breast,
still thick with burning scars.

patching differences

as time stands still
on the silent
marble wings
forever ensnared in
flowing spring
we regress to sing
of many
broken dreams
dipped in
pleasure and pain
marooned between
your heaven
'n my hell

we are yet to
demystify
the small intricacies
of ignored stimuli
which we
find wrapped
in layers 'n layers
of desolate prayers
inflamed with
a peppery cologne
of certain
uncertain dares

the smell of smog
and clay
ring in the eerie silence
just like before
yet life cannot be
yesterday

let me call it march 2012

the spring blush is fading fast
and her thoughts unfetter
in a plaster cast
the pulsating silhouette is quietly
engulfed
in the lush green of the gravel path

the hills are bare
the mountains dark
the sky is smoky and the sea afar
the shore is blank
and my dreams ajar
my lifeline
stumbles upon the troubled star

the thick glass
shields my memories march
it's tough to quietly smash
the thickening dusk
nothing is true nothing lasts
i strain to search
and willfully submerge
in the anxiety of broken hearts

wait
my dear calcutta girl
i espy illusions
breeding in the dark
wimpled all over my flaming earth
maybe for a few moments
the world stops to revolve
and fails to start

the silhouette is lost and my day is bust

the old man is no more

the wingless butterfly
lies trapped,
in the uniform,
the stench of silent guns,
restores the upheaval,
and unrest of
ancient heartburns.

down below,
the tea gardens retreat,
the chain entwining
the iron gates,
groan and tarnish,
like unquenched love
in her flaming heart,
now sadly hostile.

the woodworms
crawl and wriggle,
whirr and dribble,
and tirelessly drill,
through heavy mustachios
and ancient frills,
grimly gazing yonder
over evolving thrills.

the floorboards creek,
with the heaviness
of foul breath,
and nameless misdeeds,
the lights shine no more,
the porcelains
are packed with filth,
and the mattress
shabby and stiff,
with stains of drying guilt,

sadly, the old man is gone,
and the tale is lost
from you and all.

vow

always
remind yourself
and yer breed

whether
one is in plenty
or in need

never ever
cease
to burn
your brand

or hoist
yer
mother's flag

on every
golden race
of the
human heart

stop not

till ye reclaim
every ounce
of lost pride

ruthlessly
snatched away
from yer life

by providence
and bullies
on all sides

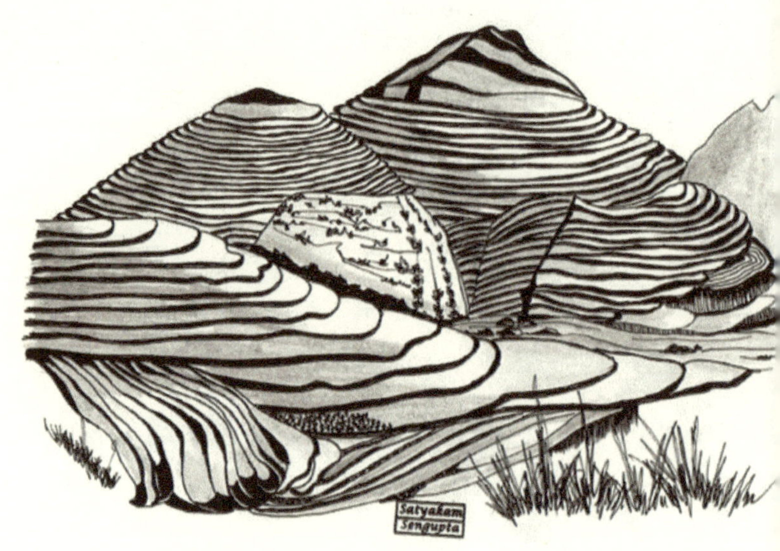
Satyakam
Sengupta

the evening blues

i browse,
through
crowded banks
of the strand,
leisurely
turning oyster red,
with swarming fires,
of unspoken
desires,
naively flooding,
the creaking pier.

flourescent
umbrellas pop up,
here, there
and everywhere,
as in bustling fanfare,
the wafting smell
of luscious fare,
thicken the sultry air,
as lovers stream in
pair by pair,
with careless flair.

the humid trickle,
never ceases
to slip down your hair,
lick your lips,
and glide down
your rear,
revving pangs,
of bygone crushes
and cares,
now spent,
though unaware.

the ripples drift,
and embrace
the tumbling leaves,
the moonlight
kisses,
the trembling breeze,
flowers enflame
my shoulders bare,
stirring
reckless aromas,
of adolescent dares.

i swear,
the evening
sweats
with obvious stares,
as hasty touches
seeks to ensnare,
trivial treasures,
which one ought not
loosen there,
though they be
in deep despair.

what measure,
weighs life's pleasure,
if every prayer
is always in favour,
and shared all over .....

impasse

the despair
springs
from deep within
to engulf
the heart 'n mind
the will to survive
is at stake
the spring breeze
stops to smile

i fumble
with my feelings dear
and cannot
make out
what is right 'n clear
the summer is
near to boil
and simmer
and destroy me
altogether

yet i would fain
stretch to feel
the cool shades
of growing
melancholy

it doesn't
help me
revive my zeal
they only help
me grieve

wanderlust

wandering
for the same
ambitions and treasures

and suffering
the same
pains and pleasures

i come to play
the same game
again and again hereafter

it is in this
wishful belief of
finding something better

i destroy myself
time and again
to recreate and re-discover

the essence
of life and evolution
tucked insidewraps and covers

i keep on
wandering
for the same aims and desires

and suffer
the same pains and pleasures
till the mystery surrenders
within me

can you say why

can you say, why
the soul
keeps on imprinting,
tiny footprints,
on the breasts
of galactic crests?

why does the mind,
keep on smiling,
crying and cursing?
why does the body,
keep on
weeping and lusting,
gluttoning,
and slaughtering?

when
it could have
noiselessly eased,
its hold,
on the good 'n bad
perceptions,
of mortal folds;

and calmly
diminished,
into eternal synergy,
within the divine
incandescence,
of the almighty.

the world at large

dare to dream

i dare
to dream
different dreams
in every resurrection

i choose
to unite seeds
of diverse beads
in endless life-lines

i learn
to gently surge
with divine purge
and bind all destinies

i weave
a complete whole
embracing all souls
in this cosmic parabole

yet at times
i bury myself
in feigned disguise
to shed the heat
of sly and scheming beasts

though i am
equally adept
in slaying hatreds
and digging graves
for all depraved

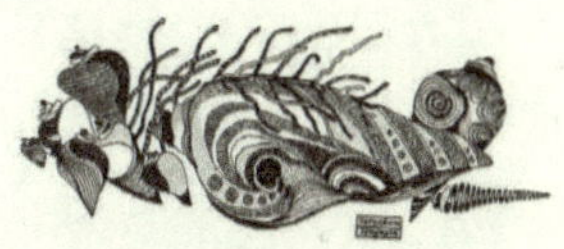

সমস্ত মানুষ স্বাধীনভাবে সমান মর্যাদা
এবং অধিকার নিয়ে জন্মগ্রহণ করে।
তাঁদের বিবেক এবং বুদ্ধি আছে
সুতরাং সকলেরই একে অপরের প্রতি ভ্রাতৃত্বসুলভ
মনোভাব নিয়ে আচরণ করা উচিত।

*"All human beings are born free and equal in dignity and rights.
They are endowed with reason and conscience
and should act towards one another in a spirit of brotherhood."*

Universal Declaration of Human Rights (Article

we have grown together

we have grown together
across borders, hills and rivers,
we grow together
even now and here,
amidst lanes and bylanes of urban desires.

but we share our ideals no more,
nor do we share our dreams and goals,
we have stopped to share
our thoughts and foods,
and thus we do not care to know,
about our livelihoods.

we are flung apart,
with grim and uneven beliefs
of ancient religions,
which we did not wield and weave,
yet, we keep on embracing,
the diktats with all our might,
as if they were the only tenets,
to encourage new life.

and someplace,
in the dim mirror of brooding time,
the vital chords of trust
have quietly slipped out of line,
over the years we have metamorphosed,
into puritans and extremists,
playing similar games
but in the guise of special names.

you wear white apparels
during your sad funerals,
we dress in white,
to solemnize our merry nuptials,
you eat with your fingers
and we dine with spoons 'n forks,
you wash your hands after every meal,
which we have willfully written off.

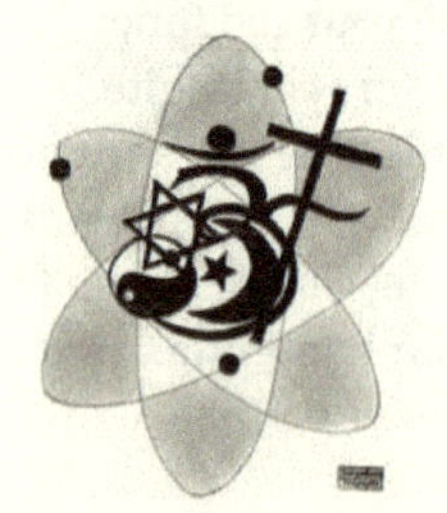

we pray seated on our bottoms,
and you pray on your knees,
you pray with palms open,
and we pray with closed ones,
he calls it the jihad,
and you call it the crusades,
while they lie trapped
in the web of a saffron brigade,
but we know for sure,
it is nothing but slaughter pure,
you know not that your ill-repute
torments for decades.

you prey on steak,
to keep yourself warm 'n strong,
yet it is sacrilege for many,
as the source is sacred,
and can't be wronged,
remember, someone said,
one man's poison is another's meat,
but a poison is a poison,
and doesn't show mercy to any.

you enforce conversion,
with bloody swords and scalpels,
we implement it subtly,
by doling out huge sums in charity,
you think you fool us every day,
but there are eyes to see,
through your cunning misdeeds,
which are but,
varying masks of tyranny.

we also watch you spread,
silent conversions in modern times,
by way of ghar wapsi,
and matrimony,
and it doesn't smell of crime!
yet, what is the use of conversion,
when we shall finally meet,
at the same sunny destination,
when all is spent and deceased.

Satyakam
Sengupta

you preserve your dead
in coffins,
while they take to cremate,
you try to protect them forever,
they reduce in ashes to forget,
however, regardless of any faith,
your beloved is your beloved,
and mine is my own -
though she be a kafir or of royal born,
yet both are fondly alike,
in the eyes of the lord!

nevertheless,
come here and stand by my side,
and look into the mirror
of trailing humankind,
are we really worlds apart?
only one is black
and the other a colourless white,
apartheid?
one may be stupid and the other bright.

but bring me
a drop of blood
which is better than another,
which shall refuse to decay,
with the passage of celestial hours;
therefore, foolish and bruised souls,
cease bragging of ruthless powers,
you are just an empty bowl,
and have nothing fine to dole.

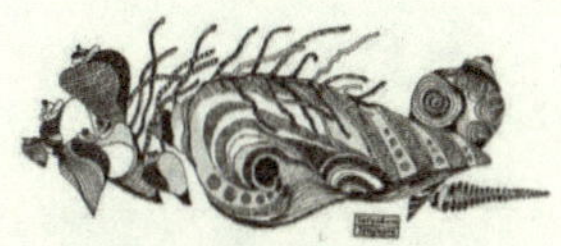

Satyakam

the essence of the mundane

i may draw my line of fate
from right to left,
and you may achieve the feat
the other way,
but does it mean,
that our souls are disparate in any way,
since when it comes to wearing shoes,
you wear the right pair
on our right toe,
and he wears the left on his left,
and never
the other way round.

therefore remember my friend,
we are all humbly born,
of the one and same quintessence,
although you may masquerade,
either as a peasant,
or a sovereign,
an honest man or a hooligan,
dream in english or else indian,
sing in chinese or africaan.

so please stop fooling
and fouling around,
and let mankind
in true harmony abound,
every life is a part of the main,
and none has the right to destroy the same.

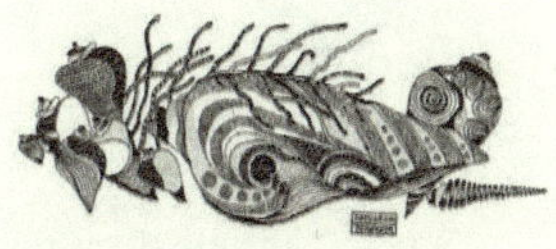

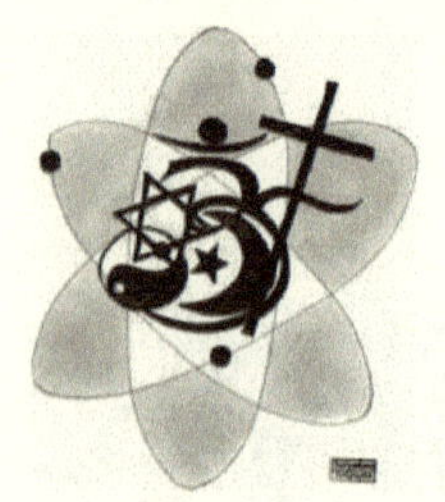

insolence

the ever-consuming
flames
of arrogant self-esteem
restrain us
from devising
the perfect dream

snuffing out
the pristine glow
of the universal flow
of love
and harmony

unleashing
a raw vitality
of frenzied lunacy
to vanquish
the basic tenets
of liberty
and human integrity

and sadly
incinerating
all likely
opportunities
of integrating with
the ultimate reality

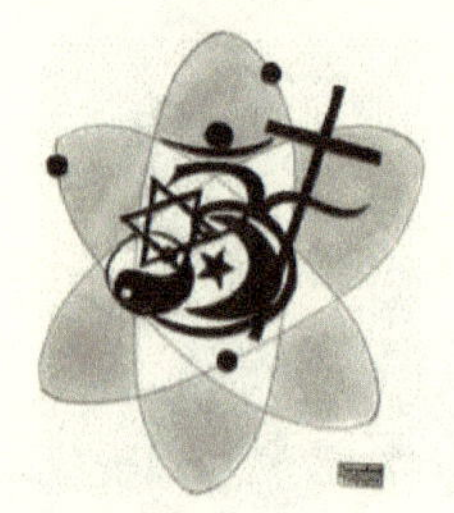

the riddle

this
senseless breeze
never stops blowing
across cosmic eons
scattering
conflicting
'n dark emotions -
of holy
beliefs'n disbeliefs

the lamp of wisdom
flickers
from one century
to another
yet right from wrong
becomes
hard to decipher

we still sway
within
everyday extremes
of truth
and blasphemy
and to cover our
ugly misdeeds
we quietly wipe out
large chunks
of humanity

it's futile exploring
learned
parchments
of faith and antiquity
and quarry
for buried knowledge
to weave 'em
into realities

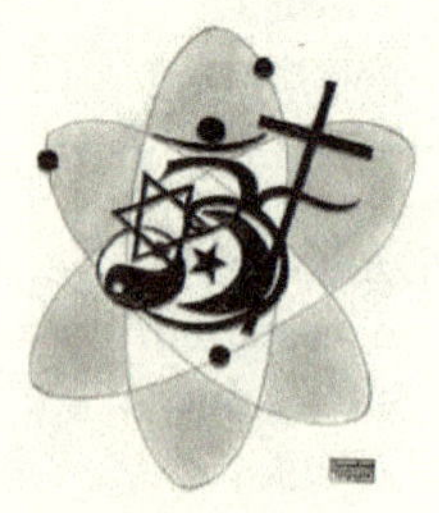

we still fail to teach
simple lessons
of freedom
and friendship
to self-indulgent
communities

it just doesn't work
anymore

the void in the mind
rears evil offshoots
to revive
bloody clashes
of warring boots

void is void
after all
and the essence of love
is precariously lost
in the confusion
of this frantic discord

yet shall we stop
to strive
and stop
to usher good in our lives

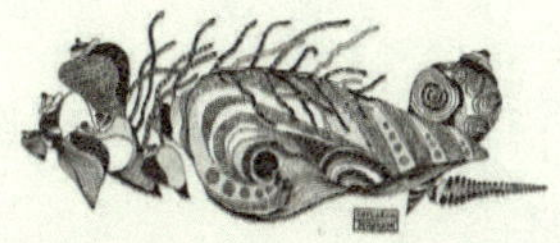

Satyakam
Sengupta

the pleasure of speculation

love, what is it,
that makes the moments
merrily sway,
at the close of every frantic day,
and at the pleasant onset,
of a mysterious high,
stirring up the evening sky.

confusion, what is it,
that arises
from stifled gestations,
of conflicting emotions,
throwing open myriad gates,
of demons and elves,
softly mystifying our selves.

intimacy, what is it,
that we always miss to see,
quietly being flung away
in the deep,
and then suddenly realise,
that life's little relationships,
are mutually dependent
on every human beat.

delight, what is it,
that helps life
move ahead eternally,
and the more
the lady is pampered,
love soaks and bewilders,
and the more
she showers her love on me,
i raise a toast to Him in glee.

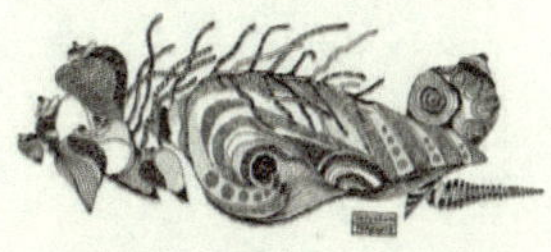

the language survives

but then again,
what can a handful
of bongalees bargain,
when the maximum lot
we cultivate,
are emotional dunces
and politically blown;

how long can we survive,
with the fading halo,
of grand ol' men
and scribes,
now, there is no firewood
left to light,
the sinking supplies,
of intellect and enterprise;

as of now,
we insatiably embark upon,
books, biryani, and hilsa
buying marathons,
in city centres,
and numerous malls,
while the gaping hollow,
becomes hard to fill and stall;

and so,
the revered tribe and creed,
branded as the
bongalee hindees,
has begun to lag behind,
with nothing fine to relish,
'n bring pride,
it wouldn't be a surprise
if they silently
retire and vanish from sight.

perhaps,
the language may survive
and crawl,
out of the cold,
of their doomsdays hall,
as it is equipped,
enriched and fireballed,
by some of
the greatest visionaries,
of the world.

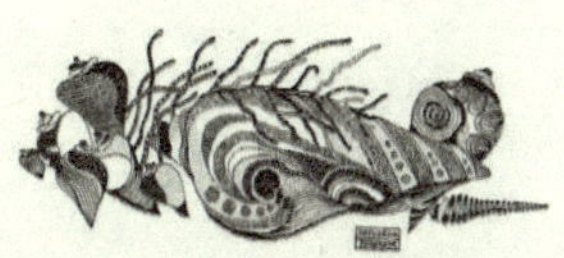

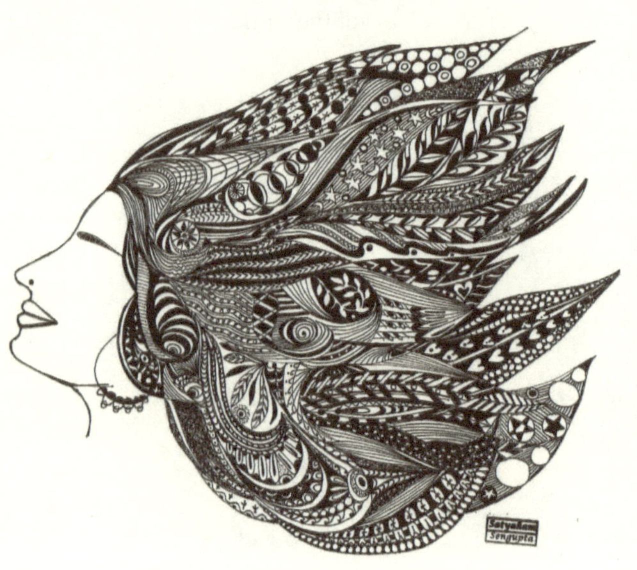

passing breeze

beautiful,
ah yes beautiful!
beautiful inspires beautiful dreams,
and beautiful shall
i pen with ease,
why shouldn't i say 'n sing beautiful,
when beautiful is all i see;

dreams,
that you fondly dream,
always do not
come for free,
however, every soul is blessed
with a certain degree;
if you have the will to persevere and see,
then do step in and tell it to me;

come,
help me heal you,
i'm always ready,
but can our amity remain ever-steady?
for now, we'd rather leave it to fickle time
to decide,
whether we can mutually reside;

feeling great, o you should!
i can make you feel even greater too,
if only i could gently fuse,
my reckless wishes,
with reality true;
and flatter
my vain flower,
to bow to my entreaties anew.

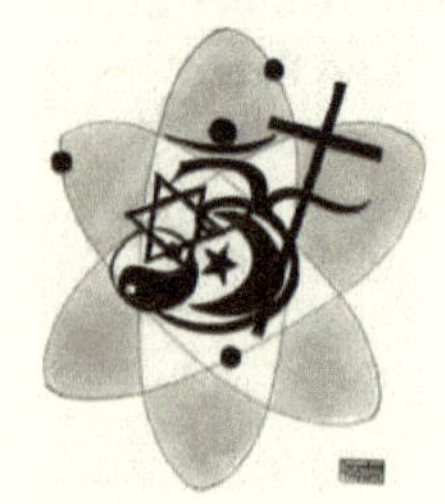

the missing dimension

she plays
and smiles in her sleep
she chuckles
and sometimes weeps
yet her tiny fingers
firmly hold onto mine
and a new dimension
adds colour to life

restoring
wagonloads of
busted promises
and lost time
which i assumed
i shall never find
'cause i have walked away
a thousand miles
to forget
and do something
worthwhile

but it seems
i'm finally
round the bend
which unerringly
defends
the eventual answer
of that nameless game

the spark in her eyes
erases all doubt
and i know
she is the one
who shall make us proud

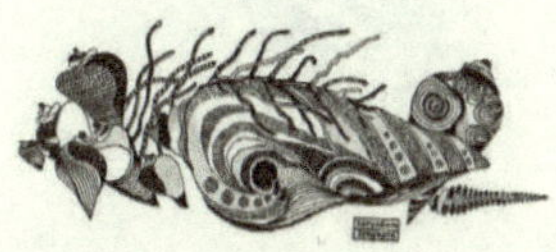

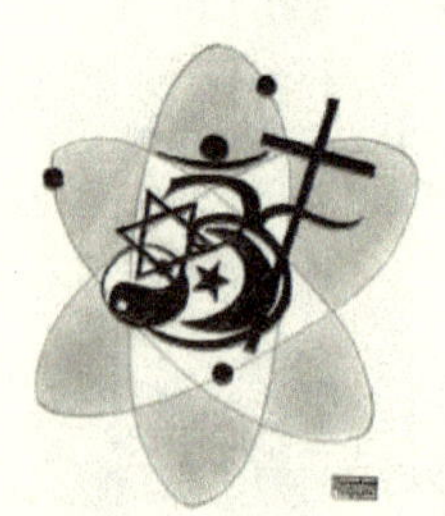

unconcealed

the frigid hours,
sail in silence,
by my window sill,
alas,
life is nothing,
but a stupid drill;

i believe,
somewhere,
sometime,
this uneven contest,
shall certainly cease;

and then,
i need not see,
the selfish
swindle and fight,
to brighten
their futures overnight;

the polite,
shudder
and freeze,
to piteously stoop,
and suffer the fright;

at times,
it surely seems,
life's quiet
'n unforeseen luck,
always goes bust,
when love is lost,
in the
human heart.

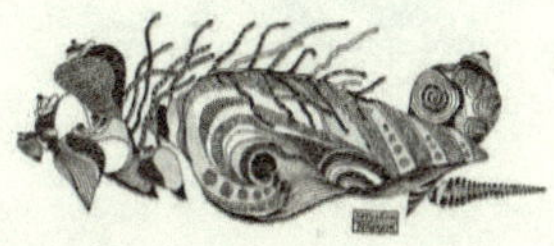

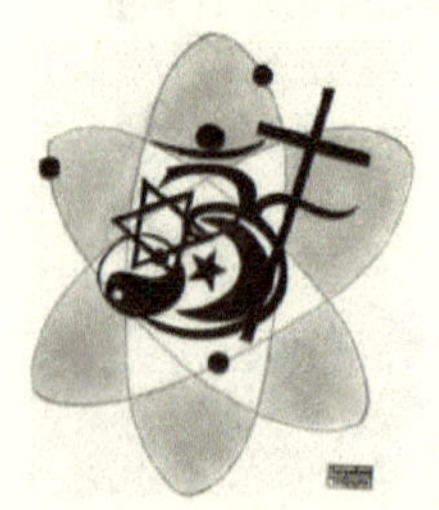

nothing is old & nothing new

nothing is old,
and nothing new,
it is just
a figment of time,
cheating you;

smeared either
with the blast,
of a fading past,
or the present,
cased in a
confused cast,
or else,
a make-believe
hereafter,
which shall
never outlast;

nothing begins,
and nothing lasts,
it is just
a figment of time,
playing
its cosmic part.

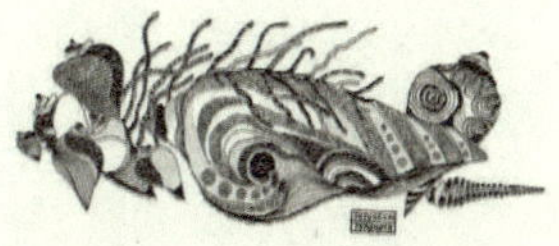

a story of moments

the child that clings,
to its mother's apron strings,
one day leaves,
is it peeved, or is it a lusty drive,
that makes it strive,
however, it reminds,
that separation always thrives.

the plaintive waves
lashing at the shore,
never realize its wishful lore,
there is still time,
to slow down and recognize,
that all our dreams
cannot always be idealized.

the joys that hover,
and swim in the air,
awash with life's gusty flair,
suddenly succumb,
to the dying wind,
remember, good times are rare,
and always hard to rewind.

the flower and the bee,
that spent life collectively,
as a queen and a doting devotee,
would also age and perish,
just like we,
before there is enough time,
to recline and cherish.

the silence of moments,
only stay enshrined,
nothing is yours and nothing mine,
so don't you weep come with me,
and let us all the pleasures sweep,
before impulsive moments,
flounder 'n cheat.

anonymous

they are still there,
six feet beneath
the thin line,
splitting the earth and air,
stripped o' flesh, and life-giving blood.

their badges of courage,
dank and smoky,
their golden epaulets, red and grimy,
their sparkling dreams,
scattered all over,
their stolen kisses,
battered and bartered,
and the song of life forever shattered.

every now and then,
weary wishes reach out,
to touch the sublime,
and try to grab the missing strands,
of windswept time,
to reinstate,
sweet-old lost primes.

yet cautious time,
neither share dreams,
nor fairy rhymes,
and compassion is bereft,
of it's might 'n lines,
it fails to soothe and soften,
age-old wounds,
that torment 'n haunt quite often.

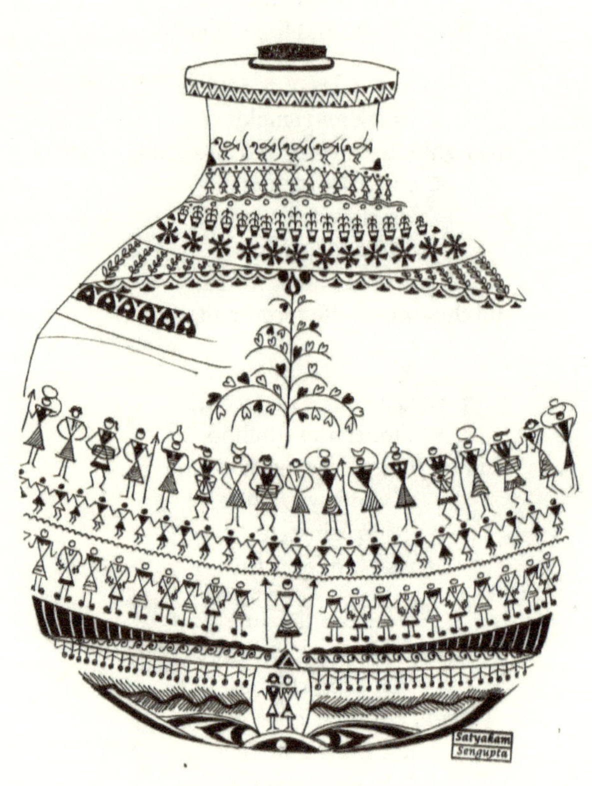

Satyakam
Sengupta

love's labour lost

reveries of love and care,
now dotingly
surround her air,
she is anxiously charmed,
at the nudge of a new sun,
invading her
quiet'n blossoming farm,
she learns to bear pain
and fear,
with suppressed
smiles and tears.

and then,
one windswept night,
apprehension
concern and fright,
furrows her brow
and merry sight,
she expectantly shivers,
to recline
on the cold-white covers,
as the night of labour,
eventually rolls over.

she timidly reaches out,
and clutches
at the sudden assault,
of bitter-sweet creation;
this is her first foray,
inside the unseen array
of brutal time,
which is forever blind,
and she knew not the laws,
of survival
on a hospital floor.

there was none
to soothe her trauma,
and soften the thick mass
of looming horror,
the nurse on duty,
was outside the door,
gleefully rapt
in secret mores,
and the medic was
only too weary,
to keep a score
on such paltry chores.

the daughter pleaded,
wept and screamed,
and went bereft;
yet the torment,
lingered unchecked,
throughout a night
which painfully bled,
she passed out
as if in death,
and snuffed out bitterly,
was the promise,
of new breath.

hopeless age

increasing age
refuses to taste,
the ginseng paste,
even at nostalgia's kind behest,

it denies to rise,
and stage a fight,
to even briefly recreate,
a semblance of lost delight,

the old man is gone,
and the tale is swept,
beneath forsaken walls,
of the villa in shambles'n forlorn,

fine memoirs
are suddenly torn,
and bits of infancy
slowly deform,
and become irreparably timeworn,

the cold 'n slimy night,
is still wedged astride,
the cold sweat of mortal fright,
and avaricious ghosts
of naked strife.

the hollow within

beneath the
tapering beams
of a mid-day sun,
encircled lavishly,
with fading beats
of drifting jungle drums,
it wrestled,
with all its might,
to tear through
the bleeding plight,
of incessant time;
airless, dark,
and devoid of shine.

undoubtedly,
blessed is existence,
spawning new life,
yet cursed
be infancy,
as it begins in strife.

it sets out,
with nothing bright,
and after toiling hard,
with all its might,
'n staging countless fights,
achieving targets
day and night,
ends up with nothing bright;
cause he can't carry
nothing,
beyond this life.

the curse

the tree of life,
has grown meek and weak,
hopelessly clutching
the yielding bricks,
of perished family deeds,
the partition
has taken its toll,
and your ancestral hall,
is under someone
else's scroll.

sadly, the other day
we met a fool on our way
who rudely jeered to say,
that after the 47's
divisive days,
their merry soil was preyed,
with more runaway zamindars,
than zamins
on Padma's eastern bay.

but will he ever know,
that even
a tiny measure of earth,
beneath your rusty throne,
is your own,
and entirely your own;
and none has the right,
to forcibly make you disown.

so my son,
don't lose your calm,
though the show
may remain unsung,
let there be no breach of trust,
even from the tiny pores
of your crust,
we must recreate,
the glory of the luminous past.

but, then again,
this same old selfish friend,
did not stop at being vain,
'cause he has been tutored
to devise,
many silly questions,
covering this massacre,
despite the torment
and despair it promptly ushers.

he puffs up
his vainglorious pride,
and harshly snaps to deride,
the cowardice of zamindars,
who failed to defy,
and put up a dying fight,
after all - the zamin,
was their birthright.

but go tell him yee,
that there were more
martyrs than men,
on Padma's eastern glen,
therefore,
friend, never get piqued,
by such comments,
allow no fool to toss a jibe,
at your ruinous plight.

tell them,
loud and clear,
as well as forthright,
though the catastrophe,
left many high and dry,
none could snatch
away their pride,
now, they are scattered worldwide,
and they shall struggle
and survive.

farewell sir

we never knew,
you shall go away so soon,
the way you chose,
you have taken away
with grandiose,
the load of your life,
on your light-winged stride,
as you had rightly surmised,
you have disappeared
like a seraph,
without anyone's consent,
or soliciting any prize.

we had often
argued with zest, to profess,
that shouldn't
your dreams and memoirs,
find a quiet breathing space,
or else lie scattered
in golden letters,
in abundance,
and without fetters,
which should forever shine
under the sun,
else glimmering moonlight,
to offer sublime insight,
in times
of distress, as well as plight.

i heard him say

my memories don't hold sway,
on my psyche any more, anyway,
i believe they should quietly move away,
with my exit and without much delay,
my memoirs shall not burden,
the freedom of my children,
and pose a hurdle in their survival,
unless, there is a definite bargain
from its frequent recital ...

amusingly,
this uneven stretch of years,
has been an open 'n glorious sphere,
bedecked with varied souvenirs;
i have played my bit of hide 'n seek,
and have reached a point in life,
where i see the day get dark,
even before the advent of night,
where men are openly traded and crucified,
and dogs worshipped and glorified ...

nonetheless,
it was by some chance ruse,
else the legacy of a mysterious muse,
which helped me to eventually diffuse,
the rift between the good and bad,
without facing much blues,
today, i have none to blame or praise
'cause my days glow with a steady blaze,
as i leave it upon Him to appraise,
and willingly evade all trace ...

the last denial

i bartered
the shining gold,
of my glowing years,
with dimming chandeliers,
of the present,
my dear;

just to
persuade you,
to forgive and forget,
and soothe your blazing tears;

i'm sorry,
i could not offer,
the sweet and shining glory,
of another daughter;

who always
assured to return,
but failed to step out of the urn,
and express her intention,
to board the ark,
at the last u-turn;

spirits are perhaps,
deeply soaked, in holy balm,
and need not always,
yearn to return.

Satyakam
Sengupta

unruly wishes

the dead are there,
swarming the thick air,
closely evaluating,
our intense
wishes and prayers;

they perpetually stoop,
over twilight cottage roofs,
to ring
quiet warning bells,
at the altar
of fading principles;

however,
wishes never cease
to seek,
and explore the deep,
even though they are buried,
under the dead-weight
of aging time;

quite often,
they shrink to seep,
inside strange impulses,
contests and deeds,
trying hard to re-establish,
glorious insights;

but now, nobody listens,
yet wishes deny
to accept and abstain.

being human

i no more stumble
on any heady
concoction;

to help me
softly disentangle,
from the
sweeping glow,
of the
holy mantle;

to lift me up
mortally,
from
incessant nights,
of spiritual follies;

i no more
stretch,
my heaviness,
to tread on that elfin,
yet uneasy step;

and touch
coincidence,
in between,
the freedom of
consecutive deaths;

yet i believe,
i hear
a whisper,
'bout the hideout,
of the
earthly nectar,

but i haunt,
the grounds
no more,
though the freeze
has thawed,

instead,
i leap
in the wilderness,
strewn with ignorance,
and pristine bliss.

22 shrabon 1422

i am exalted,
to call him my Sire,
'cause he is a spark of the rarest fire,
which did pierce the british ire,
by snubbing the Nobel's
bright attire.

though alas,
the glory is stolen and lost,
and has become some ruffian's consort,
and we sit like impotent nincompoops,
doing nothing but blaming
unknown dupes.

but what can you do,
when we foster among ourselves,
asses 'n fools,
who have the cheek to rashly profess,
that our Sire was inadvertently blessed,
with the glitter of a Nobel laureate.

'cause they say,
that my Sire was the first
among the oppressed,
to lay bare his lyrical best,
to the greats of the flourishing west,
who had never-ever assessed,
the sweet 'n universal lyrical spread,
the bongs of the orient possessed.

an evening to remember

the busted slits
of my skylight show,
a barren hush,
smugly nestled
beyond my hapless door,
as after the cessation
of a mighty war;

i watch
the naked posture,
of the forlorn tree,
heeding neither wind
nor weather,
grieving
for more and more,
for survival is its only lore;

why does man
fret and fall,
why does man
maim and maul,
the hungry and depressed
and the small;

why do we
perpetually run,
and hunt for fleeting fun,
why do we struggle
our very best,
to bestow promises,
which we never address;

my Mother,
mutely digests all;

yet how long shall She stall,
our brutal brawls,
breaching all fervent calls
of sanity.

www.ingramcontent.com/pod-product-compliance
Lightning Source LLC
Chambersburg PA
CBHW022001150726
47990CB00002B/552